INSIDE YOUR
MIND

Fulphil Publishing

979-8-9877411-6-0 Inside Your Mind, Paperback
979-8-9877411-4-6 Inside Your Mind, eBook
Copyright © 2023 by Fulphil Publishing

Maya Litvak (Author)
Fulphil Students (Author)
Tiffany Yau (Contributor, Editor)
Geethika Koneru (Contributor, Illustrator)
Yubin Huh (Illustrator)
Carla Alonzo (Foreword)

Published September 2023

ACKNOWLEDGMENTS

We extend our heartfelt thanks to the exceptional Fulphil team for their unflagging and enthusiastic work on this curriculum. Special acknowledgment is due to our summer 2022 interns: Katherine Muccio, Nyah Perez, Jincheng Zhao, Lilah Epstein, Brandon Choi, Shaan Patel, and Jumi Park. Your passion and dedication has been not only inspiring but also vital. This critical project would not have come to fruition without your contributions.

Additionally, we express our gratitude to Tiffany Yau, Carla Alonzo, Gulsun Cavusoglu, and Paula Martins. Your invaluable encouragement and guidance were instrumental throughout the development of this curriculum and book.

TABLE OF CONTENTS

Foreword

Written by: Carla Alonzo

Envision a world where mental health discourse permeates every household, where children are educated early, and adults candidly share their struggles. Picture a society in which we collectively benefit from shared experiences, eliminating feelings of isolation or shame.

That world has yet to materialize, but it is within reach — *Inside Your Mind* is a stepping-stone toward that goal. For individuals like me, this book has a profound impact.

Born into a family devoid of mental health understanding, my perceptions of depression and anxiety were steeped in shame and silence.

As a teenager wrestling with mental health issues, resilience was my mandate, emotional suppression my strategy, and prioritizing others' needs my default. How different things might have been if my mother had understood my experience! Unbeknownst to her, I was grappling with anxiety and depression. With no safe harbor for discussion, I maintained the facade of normalcy.

Years later, having experienced the loss of a child, I continued to remain mute. In turn, I suffered more anxiety attacks than I care to recall.

Eventually, it took a cancer diagnosis to face my emotions and seek the help I so desperately required. This battle with cancer provided a pathway to mental healing, emotional care, and self-love.

Now, I am committed to providing the support I wish had been extended to me. It has been my pleasure to work with Fulphil—the education nonprofit that has published and distributed this content—to build the curriculum my organization uses, and to continue to accessibly distribute it to schools to fuel this vision. This is the essence of this book—it demystifies mental health, promotes self-care, and aids in fostering mental health conversations within your circles.

Introduction

Written by: Maya Litvak

"Your mental health is everything – prioritize it. Make the time like your life depends on it, because it does." — *Mel Robbins, Author of The 5 Second Rule and The High 5 Habit*

1. The Goal of This Book

In this book, we are thrilled to present a comprehensive exploration of mental health — its challenges, historical development, future advancements, and more. While the subject may seem intimidating, we've demystified its concepts to ensure accessibility and comprehension.

Through *Inside Your Mind*, we aspire to inspire proactive advocacy for mental health and equip you with tools to integrate healthy practices into your life.

This book is inspired by one of the many courses that has been created by Fulphil, a nonprofit that creates equitable and inclusive education content to build compassion. *Inside Your Mind* is based on the mental health curriculum we created at Fulphil with the goal of normalizing mental health discussions and eradicating stigma. *Inside*

Your Mind, like all our other books and courses, is created by and for students. The content of this book was co-created by me, Maya Litvak, under the guidance of Tiffany Yau and mental health experts and practitioners, in addition to our esteemed colleagues, Katherine Muccio, Nyah Perez, Jincheng Zhao, Lilah Epstein, Brandon Choi, Shaan Patel, and Jumi Park—all of whom have deep theoretical and practical expertise in the sectors of psychology, wellness, sociology, and education.

I'm very proud of the thoughtfulness that has gone into creating this book, and we hope to help you embrace self-acceptance and cultivate the self-love and compassion you extend to others. Everyone—including our most admired role models—traverses unique mental health journeys. There's no need for silence or solitude in our feelings. Fortunately, shared human experiences can provide solace. Never hesitate to seek support from a peer, parent, or medical professional! Remember, mental health care is individualized—always prioritize what's best for you.

2. Section Introductions

Chapter 1: Mental Health & Wellness: Past, Present, & Future

Curious about the nature of mental health and wellness? Intrigued by their evolving definitions? In chapter 1, we journey through these concepts' historical transformations and future trajectories. We'll explore their dynamic, ever-changing role in maintaining our balance, functionality, and overall health.

Chapter 2: Mental Health Has Many Shades

In chapter 2, we'll explore the vast spectrum of mental health. We'll discuss the diverse moods we experience, the language we use to describe them, their intensity, and their non-linearity. We'll also emphasize that mental health is not a one-size-fits-all concept and discuss its variations, especially among different ethnic minority communities. Finally, we'll explore mental health in various settings, such as workplaces and schools.

Chapter 3: Checking In With Yourself And Others

We often hear advice like "make sure to check in on yourself" or "always ask your friends how they're feeling," but what do these phrases mean? In this chapter, we'll delve into the process of checking in, its importance, and the various forms it can take. We aim to equip you to become an effective mental health advocate.

Chapter 4: Being Compassionate Toward Yourself And Others

After gaining a solid understanding of mental health and wellness, we tackle the pivotal questions: How can I improve my mental health? How do I cope when my mental health is suffering?

In this chapter, we'll discuss the role of compassion, how to extend and receive it, and its various forms. We'll underscore the importance of self-compassion and supporting others when their mental health is challenged. Finally, we'll remind you that mental health is a journey, not a destination, and discuss proactive steps to enhance it.

Beyond these chapters, we have additional resources — including our cheat code recap, glossary, cited sources, and downloadable worksheet activities—that can help supplement your learning experience. If you are interested in teaching this to a class or group, we also have turnkey slideshows available for download on our website that our team and teachers across the country have vetted.

There's a wealth of knowledge awaiting us—let's dive in!

Chapter 1
Mental Health & Wellness: Past, Present, & Future

Written by: Maya Litvak and Katherine Muccio

"What mental health needs is more sunlight, candor, and more unashamed conversation." – Glenn Close, American Actress

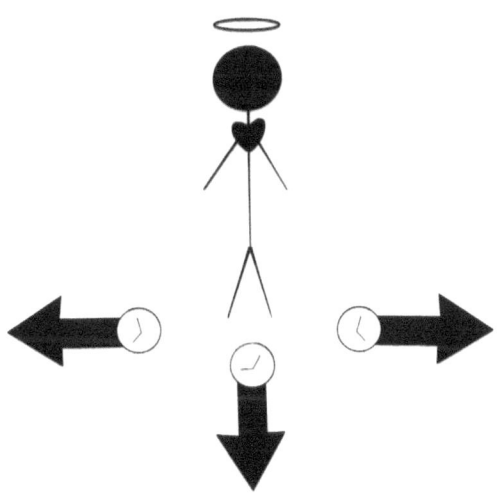

1. About: What is Mental Health & Wellness?

What is mental health? You've likely heard the term – perhaps from a teacher, your parents, or in the media. It's a vital concept for our everyday functioning.

Mental health encompasses our emotional, psychological, and social well-being, influencing how we think, feel, and act. It enables us to manage stress, form relationships, and make decisions. Consequently, mental health plays a critical role in our overall health.

No single cause or straightforward explanation exists for the development of our mental health. Factors such as genetics, brain chemistry, life experiences, substance use, culture, and interpersonal relationships all contribute.

Poor mental health correlates with poorer health outcomes, such as higher mortality rates and cardiovascular issues, reflecting a bidirectional relationship wherein each affects the other. For instance, chronic health conditions increase the likelihood of mental health problems and vice versa. Importantly, poor mental health does not necessarily equate to mental illness.

Conversely, good mental health correlates with **well-being, a state characterized by comfort, health, and happiness**. Like mental health, there are no individual determinants of well-being. Instead, it depends on genetics, social, and psychological factors. Positive emotions may be heritable to some extent. Psychological factors include personality traits like optimism, extraversion, and self-esteem, while sociocultural influences involve supportive relationships, economic status, and societal structures.

Mental Health Over Time

Now that we understand what mental health is, let's consider how it can change over time. Much like our personal growth, **mental health is a dynamic journey that evolves across our lifetime, depending**

on various internal and external factors. Stressful situations, like undertaking a rigorous academic workload, can potentially degrade mental health.

Why Teach Good Mental Health?
As you may surmise, good mental health is vital for our quality of life and everyday functioning, making its promotion crucial.

Good mental health equips us to handle stress effectively, underpins our physical health, nurtures supportive relationships, fosters a sense of meaning, and bolsters our self-image.

2. The Origins and Evolution of Mental Health & Wellness

Past: The History of Mental Health & Wellness[1]
Given that mental health is inherent to all human life, it has been present for ages.

In some cultures, mental health and wellness were always of high importance. For instance, practitioners of Ayurveda in India sought the balance of the human body, mind, and spirit, emphasizing aspects such as nutrition, physical activity, sleep quality, moderation, ethical behavior, and positive emotions – mirroring contemporary concepts of mental health.

However, in the United States, it wasn't until post-Civil War that "mental hygiene" was coined and began to gain interest. Poor mental

---

[1]   Bertolote, Jose. "The Roots of the Concept of Mental Health." World Psychiatry 7, no. 2 (2008): 113–16. https://doi.org/10.1002/j.2051-5545.2008.tb00172.x.

hygiene, or mental deviations, were predominantly considered biologically rooted, possibly due to unsuccessful genetic mutations.

By the 20th century, mental hygiene was increasingly associated with psychological and sociocultural factors. In 1948, the World Health Organization (WHO) officially recognized mental health, although a universally accepted definition remains elusive. Even with WHO's acknowledgment, negative attitudes have persisted, contributing to ongoing stigmatization.

Stigmatization of Different Disorders[2]
Despite acknowledgment of mental health's existence, those suffering from poor mental health often face negative perceptions and ostracization.

How an individual views mental health largely hinges on their beliefs about its origins. In the past, poor mental health was often seen as a punishment or demonic possession, leading to hostility towards sufferers. Conversely, Hippocrates posited that an individual's mental health was influenced by their life circumstances and environment, refraining from vilifying sufferers as "evil" or "inhumane."

Present: The Importance of Mental Health & Wellness Today
Why should mental health matter to you, decades later? Because when we are at our best, we can live at our best. Our self-perceptions

---

[2] Bornstein, Jeffrey. "Stigma, Prejudice and Discrimination against People with Mental Illness." Stigma, Prejudice and Discrimination Against People with Mental Illness. American Psychiatry Association, August 2020. https://www.psychiatry.org/patients-families/stigma-and-discrimination#:~:text=A%202017%20study%20involving%20more,after%20one%20and%20two%20years.

and self-talk are significant. You are valuable, you are important – so behave accordingly! Prioritize your mental health; invest in yourself!

Consider this: every year, you visit the doctor for a check-up. They assess your heart rate, measure your blood pressure, and ensure that you're in peak condition. Shouldn't your mental health receive similar attention? The well-being of your mind is as crucial as your physical health. A content, healthy mind drives us to pursue and achieve our goals!

In the present day, mental health is receiving increased attention. Prioritizing mental health has become a significant concern for many Americans. Over the latter half of the 20th century, lectures, organizations, and social media marketing campaigns intended to stimulate conversation around mental health have multiplied and continue to grow in popularity.

This focus on mental health arises due to the escalating prevalence of mental illness in the United States. As of 2019, approximately one in five Americans are living with a mental illness, a statistic that rises each year. Additional support is essential!

Our aim should be to focus on prevention and increase access to mental health treatment and services. Ensuring that individuals receive the help they need and that we all contribute is paramount. Even reaching out to a friend, though it may seem insignificant, can make a world of difference.

Furthermore, the dialogue surrounding mental health must continue to evolve. Mental illness need not remain a taboo topic. Those who may be struggling should feel comfortable sharing their experiences and feel free to express their vulnerability. Let a friend know you're there for them. Let's help normalize the conversation!

The Evolution of the Stigmatization of Mental Health[3]

While mental health has become a more openly discussed topic today, a considerable stigma still surrounds it. What is stigma? **Stigma** refers to the act of viewing someone negatively due to a particular characteristic or attribute, which could range from skin color, or culture, to disability. In the context of mental health, stigma emerges when an individual is viewed negatively solely because they have a mental illness.

The term "stigma" was first introduced as a scientific concept by psychologists in the 1960s, based on the definition provided by sociologist Erving Goffman.

However, stigma has existed for centuries. There is a long history of prejudice and discrimination against individuals with mental illness. [4]For millennia, society treated those suffering from mental disorders akin to criminals, subjecting them to imprisonment, torture, and execution. During the Middle Ages, mental illnesses were perceived as divine punishments, with those afflicted believed to be possessed by evil spirits.

While stigma varies according to culture, society, and specific disorders, it is also a universal human experience.

As we navigate through the 21st century, persistent stereotypes associated with mental health stigma persist. Currently, those with

---

[3]　"Stigma and Discrimination." Mental Health Foundation, October 4, 2021. https://www.mentalhealth.org.uk/explore-mental-health/a-z-topics/stigma-and-discrimination.

[4]　"Stigma, Discrimination and Mental Illness." Better Health Channel. Department of Health; Human Services, September 18, 2015. https://www.betterhealth.vic.gov.au/health/servicesandsupport/stigma-discrimination-and-mental-illness.

mental illnesses are often perceived as dangerous, unpredictable, and unreliable. The stigma surrounding mental health remains pervasive and prominent in society, transcending various walks of life. These are widespread, yet mistaken beliefs.

Interestingly, modern society largely remains oblivious to this stigmatization. This lack of recognition can be harmful to those with mental illnesses, highlighting the importance of individual and collective responsibility in educating ourselves, raising awareness, speaking up, and advocating for those who may struggle to do so. It's time to step up as an ally!

Yet, hope remains! Numerous people are actively engaged in combating these biases and shifting this narrative. There are individuals, clubs, groups, and large organizations committed to dismantling these stereotypes. People are expanding their understanding and fostering open-mindedness. You can spearhead this change! By participating in this course, you're taking a step in the right direction.

Mental Health in the 21st Century[5]

The landscape of mental health in the 21st century differs substantially from the past. Mental illnesses are more prevalent now than ever before, particularly among teenagers and young adults in the U.S. For instance, the percentage of adolescents (ages 12-17) who experienced at least one Major Depressive Episode has been on the rise—as of 2021, it reached 20.1%. Consequently, there is an unprecedented demand for psychiatrists, treatments, and support services.

---

[5] "The State of Mental Health in America." Mental Health America. Accessed June 12, 2022. https://mhanational.org/issues/state-mental-health-america.

Regrettably, over half of Americans with mental illnesses remain untreated. This equates to over 27 million people not receiving the assistance they require. For many, treatment is informal. Individuals often seek support from family, friends, teachers, guidance counselors, or religious leaders. Less frequently, they consult a medical doctor or psychiatrist. However, we must strive to enhance the accessibility of these professionals for future needs.

Fortunately, measures are being taken to render mental health services more readily available. Despite the COVID-19 pandemic leading to worsened mental health for many, physicians and healthcare providers also capitalized on the situation as an opportunity to devise alternative and accessible treatment methods.

For instance, during the pandemic, there was a significant increase in the use of telemedicine. [6]Telemedicine refers to the provision of healthcare services remotely. This might involve using a smartphone, tablet, or computer to virtually meet with a healthcare professional.

Telemedicine has facilitated the connection of individuals to healthcare services, regardless of their location or schedule. Olympic swimmer Michael Phelps candidly discussed his mental health struggles and his coping mechanisms during the pandemic.[7] He used

---

[6]   "Technology and the Future of Mental Health Treatment." National Institute of Mental Health. U.S. Department of Health and Human Services. Accessed June 12, 2022. https://www.nimh.nih.gov/health/topics/technology-and-the-future-of-mental-health-treatment.

[7]   Marcellus, Sibile. "'Stop the Shame': Talkspace, Michael Phelps, Demi Lovato Battle against Mental Illness Stigma." Yahoo! News, May 21, 2021. https://news.yahoo.com/stop-the-shame-michael-phelps-demi-lovato-and-online-therapy-platform-fight-mental-illness-stigma-124714145. html?guccounter=1&guce_referrer=aHR0cHM6Ly93d3cuZ29vZ2xlLmNvbS8&guce_referrer_sig=AQAAABbm6WZtI0sglcn0fBx02nG-

Talkspace, an online and mobile therapy company, to conduct virtual therapy sessions with counselors and psychiatrists.

However, in the contemporary world, prioritizing mental health isn't an exclusive concern of Olympic swimmers or celebrities. You are the best judge of your mental state. You know when it's time to take a breather, step back, and prioritize your well-being. Don't hesitate to speak up and seek help! Remember, you are not alone, and you don't require a formal diagnosis to access support.

Mental Health in the Media[8]

With the advent of social media and technology in the 21st century, discourse around mental health is surfacing everywhere on our screens! An array of individuals, including teenagers, celebrities, influencers, parents, athletes, singers, and activists, are utilizing their platforms for the greater good. From Instagram posts and stories to TikTok videos, conversations about mental health are escalating. Many posts aim to educate people not only on the concept of mental health, but also on how to act as an ally and support both oneself and others.

Remember, no matter what challenges you face or experiences you undergo, you are never alone. You possess the strength to speak up. Let your voice resonate.

---

eLe1zHLjoqLfQ3TMgxXhgjCqJvbi98c-x_NcPZWjxDqZWe0FAlcuDlIPJd
FAOhWo2KxOEKvHHAPzXyr9H02ysgYKGqMxpHsC8kjG2a
W0BWYlz6u8D6PUEfgs4ABCHaeVmqHOa_f5Lopl2Fb0YIoy.

[8] "#StatusOfMind: Social Media and Young People's Mental Health and Wellbeing." Young Health Movement. RSPH | Royal Society for Public Health UK, May 2017. https://www.rsph.org.uk/static/uploaded/d125b27c-0b62-41c5-a2c0155a8887cd01.pdf.

Singer and actor Joshua Bassett is one individual using his platform to foster positivity. Through his music, social media presence, and interviews, he openly shares his struggles with mental health as a teenager coping with stress and anxiety. Consequently, he pledged to donate all the proceeds from his song "Crisis" and its accompanying merchandise to various mental health organizations, all of which are dedicated to assisting young people like himself. Bassett employs his social media to illuminate mental health resources and initiate conversation. He aims to ensure individuals have the information necessary to establish connections with those who can provide support.

Social media has become a megaphone for those using their platforms to educate, motivate, and uplift others. It has facilitated connection, reminding us that we are not alone in our thoughts and that these thoughts are widely heard and shared. Maybe you've seen such content, read it, or even created it yourself! Don't be reluctant to engage in the conversation! It's never too late to join in!

Case Study #1: Breaking Down Barriers and Increasing Access to Mental Health Services at the Click of a Button[9]
Many individuals face barriers that prevent them from accessing mental health resources, whether that be financial scarcity, fear of stigmatization, lack of geographical accessibility, or poor awareness.

Today, it is all about increasing access — meaning, the goal is to get as many people as possible the help they need.

---

[9] Pollacco, Maya. "Ariana Grande to Give Away $2 Million Worth of Therapy." 89.7 Bay, July 6, 2021. https://bay.com.mt/ariana-grande-to-give-away-two-million-worth-of-therapy/.

Maybe it's therapy, medication, or a change in diet and exercise habits. Maybe it's all the above! How can we help people gain access to these aids? Look no further than your screen!

Earlier in chapter 1, we discussed mental health in the 21st century and the emergence of virtual therapy as a tool for those seeking mental health services.

In the age of technology, it's no wonder that we can also use our phones, computers, and tablets for accessing healthcare as well.

Celebrity investors looking to promote change in the mental health space have partnered with online therapy platforms to address the access disparity.

Here is a case study of change in the making: promoting virtual therapy with a generation that is already well acquainted with the technology. It's a promising venture!

Ariana Grande Partners with E-Counseling & E-Therapy Service, BetterHelp
Indeed, pop superstar Ariana Grande announced a partnership with BetterHelp, a leading online counseling and therapy platform, in June 2021. This was communicated to her massive follower base via her Instagram account.

BetterHelp, the largest provider of online counseling services, strives to make professional therapy more accessible to individuals grappling with mental health issues. This platform enables users to virtually connect with licensed psychologists, family therapists, clinical social workers, and board-licensed professional counselors.

With this partnership, Grande has used her influence to promote mental health awareness and ensure that her fans and the wider public know that resources like BetterHelp are available to them. This collaboration is a significant step in normalizing discussions about mental health and reducing stigma, demonstrating that anyone, including celebrities, may need support at times.

Following the bombing attack on Grande's Manchester concert in 2017[10], the singer became outspoken about her own experience with PTSD and anxiety, and the importance of taking care of our mental health.

By donating over $6 million in free therapy over the past year, she hopes not only to increase access to mental healthcare but to encourage others to prioritize their mental health as well.

By signing up for BetterHelp through Grande's code, enrollees get their first month free and 15% off their second month.

---

[10] "Manchester Arena Bombed during Ariana Grande Concert." History. com. A&E Television Networks, May 18, 2018. https://www.history. com/this-day-in-history/manchester-arena-bombed-during-ariana-grande-concert.

While her donation and commitment to BetterHelp are steps in the right direction, Grande acknowledges that access to services is a much larger systemic problem. Those with insufficient access to resources and knowledge will continue to struggle if we do not act. **Therapy is not for a privileged few but should be accessible to all**.

Grande hopes BetterHelp can serve as a starting point for people to continue to build space for healing in their lives.

If you or a loved one is struggling with keeping good mental health habits, or could just use that additional support, consider trying BetterHelp or another virtual therapy platform. [11]

If you're not quite ready to seek professional help just yet, that's completely okay. It's worth taking some time to reflect, consider your options, and think it over. You might try making a list of pros and cons, discussing it with your support system, or researching more about it. While venturing outside of your comfort zone can feel intimidating, it could also be immensely rewarding.

Ariana Grande, in partnership with BetterHelp, aims to enhance access to therapy. She hopes that her efforts will inspire others to introspect on their mental health, consider therapy for the first time, dispel self-judgment or stigma, and feel more comfortable seeking help.

Take a moment to reflect on these points. If you've experienced therapy before, do you feel it had a positive effect on your mental health and altered your perception of the mental health landscape? If you haven't engaged in therapy yet, contemplate how you might impact your mental health and contribute to addressing the issues

---

[11]   "5 Companies Offering Solutions for Employee Mental Health." RSS, April 6, 2021. https://www.artemishealth.com/blog/5-companies-offering-solutions-for-employee-mental-health.

surrounding it, such as stigma and access. Remember, even the smallest action can make a big impact.

3. Future: What Mental Health Looks Like Down the Line[12]

The future of mental health is rooted in personalization. This approach not only tailors treatment plans but also emphasizes seeing the person beyond their illness. It's about adopting a more holistic, multifaceted perspective toward care. Treatment might involve medication and therapy, but it could also encompass a balanced diet, physical activities like dance breaks, or designated moments of self-care. The future of mental health is about ensuring each individual has access to the treatment and support that best suits their unique needs and circumstances.

In the late 20th century and early 21st century, major advancements have been made in the realm of medications to treat neurological disorders and mental illnesses. Today, there is an increasing emphasis on the integration of therapy and medication in treating mental health conditions.

Recognizing the interconnection between mind and body is crucial. Increasingly, there is an understanding of the significant role that nutrition and exercise play in fostering mental health and overall wellness. Looking ahead, medical professionals will likely incorporate this multifaceted view into their practice. They will approach an

---

[12]   "New Mental Health Trends and the Future of Psychiatry." Maryville Online, 2019. https://online.maryville.edu/blog/future-psychiatry/.

individual's experience with mental illness from a more holistic perspective to provide highly personalized treatment.

The Future of Mental Health and Wellness

A crucial aspect of the future of mental health and wellness involves dismantling the stigma associated with it. From eradicating toxic masculinity to challenging the perpetuation of harmful labels, we must strive to change our language, educate ourselves, and remain sensitive to the feelings and needs of others. Next time you're scrolling on your phone, seek out the candid and open conversations we've discussed. Start by initiating open dialogues with your family and friends!

The aim is to concentrate on preventing mental illness in the long run and broadening access to treatment as much as possible. We can use our smartphones not just for education but also for reaching out to professionals. Providing early support and help could be the key to reducing the prevalence of mental health issues and dismantling the associated stigma.

Technology can aid us in achieving this goal! With innovative tech developments like telehealth and virtual therapy apps on smartphones and tablets, care can be convenient, consistent, affordable, and extremely accessible! Individuals no longer need to leave the comfort of their homes for care. There is no travel time or costs and no waiting in reception rooms. It's all available at a simple click, no matter where you are!

The Importance of Learning Positive Mental Health Practices

Why prepare for your future? Why prioritize yourself and your mental health and wellness? Because you're all you've got, and you deserve the best! Take control of your own life; you have the strength and power to make it incredible! Invest time in yourself now!

The journey begins with small changes, whatever feels right to you! Perhaps it's establishing a consistent morning and night routine or taking a stress-relieving walk around the block with friends. Maybe it's about adjusting the way you talk to yourself. Practice positive self-talk or boost yourself up the way you would your best friend! Don't hesitate to give yourself a pat on the back occasionally.

Remember, a "new you" won't emerge overnight. This positive, happy, and healthy individual is already within you! Allow yourself grace, patience, and support to reconnect with them.

4. Cheat Code Recap

1. Mental health is important for our day-to-day functioning.
2. Mental health is our emotional, psychological, and social well-being that affects how we think, feel, and act.
3. There is no single cause or simple explanation for the development of our mental health.
4. Mental health and health outcomes share a bidirectional relationship, so they affect each other proportionally.
5. Good mental health is associated with an important concept called well-being, which is the state of being comfortable, healthy, or happy.
6. The history of mental health and wellbeing has evolved over time.
7. The future of mental health is personalized care.

Chapter 2
Mental Health Has Many Shades

Written by: Maya Litvak, Nyah Perez, and Jincheng Zhao

"There is no standard normal. Normal is subjective. There are seven billion versions of normal on this planet." — Matt Haig, Author

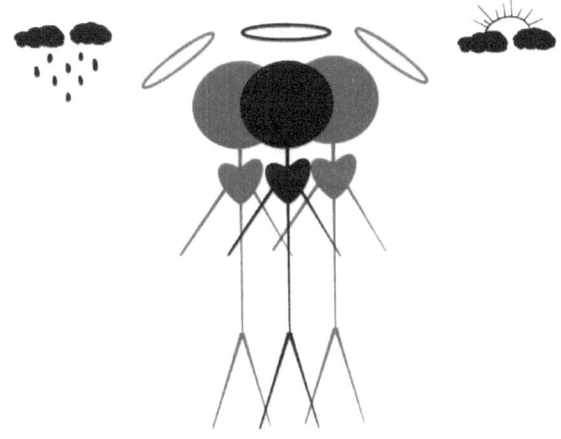

1. Spectrum of Mental Health

Mental health is an incredibly individual and diverse experience. It does not conform to a one-size-fits-all model. The mental health of an individual can also fluctuate, varying from day to day. It's important to remember that everyone has their unique narrative, and making assumptions about others should be avoided.

Mental health conditions are vast and varied, with each disorder having its own specific set of symptoms that can affect our thoughts, feelings, and behavior. While the terms "mental health" and "mental illness" are often used interchangeably, they do not carry the same meaning. "Poor mental health" and "mental illness," though interconnected, are not synonymous.

Mental health is a broad concept encompassing our thoughts, feelings, emotions, and our capacity to connect with others and ourselves. On the other hand, mental illness refers to a specific condition that affects these aspects of our lives and is diagnosed by a healthcare professional. Therefore, a person may experience poor mental health without necessarily having a diagnosed mental illness.

Understanding and tending to your mental health can pave the way for a healthier and more content life. It also equips you to identify when you might need additional support and how to seek it. We all encounter days filled with stress, perhaps due to work or academics, or periods of anxiety, like the moments leading up to a performance or presentation. Life's overwhelm can be perfectly normal, and good mental health is about navigating and coping with these challenges.

Equally crucial is to understand that good mental health isn't simply the absence of a diagnosed mental illness. Rather, it involves cultivating a healthy relationship with your mind, body, and emotions. Good mental health is about embracing resilience, balance, and emotional well-being as integral parts of your overall wellness.

2. Moods We Experience As People

Humans can experience a diverse range of emotions. In this section, we'll define certain terms associated with emotions and discuss how they differ from mental illnesses.

Disclaimer: the information provided in this chapter is solely for educational purposes and should not be used as a tool for self-diagnosis. Mental health holds as much importance as physical health. If you have any concerns or questions, please reach out to a trusted adult or a medical professional.

Term	Everyday Definition	Official Mental Illness Diagnosis
Attention-Deficit/ Hyperactivity Disorder (ADHD)	Often incorrectly viewed as a "made up" disorder present only in children, assuming all individuals are either hyperactive or lazy.	A neurodevelopmental disorder characterized by persistent patterns of inattention, hyperactivity, and impulsivity that significantly impact daily functioning and well-being.
Anxiety	Often incorrectly used to describe a state of feeling nervous or worried that something bad is going to happen.	A nervous disorder characterized by intense, excessive, and persistent worry and fear about everyday situations. Often, anxiety disorders can involve repeated episodes of sudden feelings of intense anxiety and fear or terror that reach a peak within minutes (panic attacks).

Term	Everyday Definition	Official Mental Illness Diagnosis
Depression	Often incorrectly used to describe a feeling of hopelessness, helplessness, and sadness.	A mental disorder that causes feelings of sadness and/or a loss of interest in activities you once enjoyed. It can lead to emotional and physical problems and can decrease your ability to function. Note: symptoms must be present for at least two weeks and represent a change in your previous level of functioning for a diagnosis by a mental health professional.
Post-Traumatic Stress Disorder (PTSD)	Often incorrectly used to emphasize and/or describe an experience.	A mental health condition triggered by witnessing or experiencing a terrifying event.
Bipolar Disorder	Often incorrectly used to describe a person who changes their mind or moods rapidly.	A mental disorder that causes extreme mood swings including emotional highs and lows.
Obsessive-Compulsive Disorder (OCD)	Often incorrectly used to describe an inflexible person who pursues cleanliness and routine.	A mental disorder with obsessions that are repeated, unwanted, and persistent. These thoughts or urges are often intrusive and cause distress or anxiety.

As you can see, it's crucial to understand that identifying a mental illness involves many intricate details and nuances, and should therefore be determined by a medical professional. Seek help if you feel it's necessary.

If you're diagnosed with a mental health disorder or facing mental health challenges, it's important not to fall into a pattern of self-blame, developing a victim mentality that places the fault for your struggles solely on you. This is simply not true! A victim mentality often emerges when dealing with past trauma or betrayal, particularly in the absence of a strong support network. Recognize that this mindset is an unhealthy coping mechanism that can damage your self-esteem and self-confidence. If you observe someone struggling in this manner, help them by highlighting their strengths, validating their feelings, and encouraging them to consult with a medical professional.

Try It Out!
Building upon the knowledge gathered from this section, you can attempt to devise alternative adjectives to depict emotions without using the names of mental illnesses.

For instance, rather than stating, "I'm so OCD," you could express, "I have a strong preference for organization and tidiness. Disorder tends to disturb me significantly."

This approach promotes an accurate and respectful conversation about mental health. Try it out!

3. Mental Health in Different Communities

Mental health also takes on different states in minority communities. **A minority is defined as a group that differs culturally, ethnically, or racially and doesn't constitute most of society**. Within these communities, perceptions surrounding mental health can diverge significantly, often leading to stigmatization. Furthermore, it's increasingly challenging for individuals within minority communities to access mental health care due to factors such as inaccessibility, discrimination, language barriers, insurance coverage, lack of cultural competency (the ability to understand and interact effectively with people from various cultures), and cost.

Asian Americans

Asian American mental health is often affected by the **model minority myth**.[13, 14] This myth is the perception that Asian students and workers are more successful than other minority students and workers, often pitting minority groups against one another.[15]

A tragic illustration of this is the 2007 Virginia Tech University shooting. Seung-Hui Cho, the perpetrator, was regarded as unusually quiet. As a child, he had difficulties learning English, which impeded his adaptation to his predominantly white environment. He was often a target for teasing at school. Despite Cho's apparent social isolation, his parents' success in business and his sister's graduation from Princeton presented the image of his family as the stereotypical Asian American family living the American dream. The model minority myth, a stereotype that Asian Americans are universally successful,

[13] Chou, Rosalind, and Joe R. Feagin. The Myth of the Model Minority: Asian Americans Facing Racism. 2nd ed., London, Routledge, Taylor & Francis Group, 2016.

[14] Lee, Stacey J. Unraveling the 'Model Minority' Stereotype: Listening to Asian American Youth. 2nd ed., New York City, Teachers College Press, 2009.

[15] Nishi, Koko. "Mental Health among Asian-Americans." American Psychological Association, 2012. https://www.apa.org/pi/oema/resources/ethnicity-health/asian-american/article-mental-health.

added to this illusion of "normalcy," causing Cho's warning signs of mental illness to be overlooked. The label "model minority" exerts significant pressure on Asian Americans to conform to the dominant white culture and meet its expectations.

In addition to the model minority myth, cultural values and social stigma are other factors that heavily impact the mental health of Asian Americans.

Black and African Americans

The mental health of Black and African Americans is significantly impacted by systemic racism, historical oppression, and violence. When seeking mental health care, additional barriers such as insurance coverage, cultural competency, and societal stigma are often encountered. Mental health care is deeply stigmatized within these communities, largely due to historical misdiagnoses and exploitation in scientific and medical research within the U.S.

A mere two percent of American Psychological Association members are Black or African American, reinforcing the cultural competency barrier and delaying crucial mental health care. Moreover, this demographic is less likely to receive consistent baseline care and is underrepresented in health research. Even when Black and African Americans do seek mental health care, they are less likely to be offered medication or therapy compared to the general population. While there has been some progress recently, significant work remains in improving mental health care for this community.

Due to the stigma and barriers to care, many African Americans often resort to seeking support from religious or spiritual institutions such as mosques or churches. While these institutions do provide support and a sense of community, they should not be the only avenue for mental health care.

Hispanic and Latino Americans[16]

Hispanic and Latino Americans encounter numerous barriers when seeking mental health care, including language barriers, privacy concerns, societal stigma, and systemic inequities. Further concerns arise due to immigration status and the lack of health insurance coverage for mental health care. Research reveals that in the Hispanic and Latino population, both older adults and youth are more susceptible to mental distress related to immigration and acculturation.

Acculturation, which refers to the extent to which an individual has assimilated the predominant culture of their place of residence, plays a crucial role in seeking mental health care for Hispanic and Latino Americans. While those who are more assimilated are often more willing to seek mental health services, there exists a significant divide in mental health care between first and second-generation immigrant families.

Because of privacy concerns, many Hispanic and Latino Americans may be reluctant to publicly share their problems. There's an old and common saying within these cultures, "la ropa sucia se lava en casa," which translates to "dirty laundry is washed at home." This cultural need for privacy can reinforce the stigma and shame Hispanic and

---

[16] American Psychiatric Association. (2017). Mental Health Disparities: Hispanics and Latinos. https://www.psychiatry.org/File%20Library/ Psychiatrists/Cultural-Competency/Mental-Health-Disparities/Mental-Health-Facts-for-Hispanic-Latino.pdf

Latino individuals may feel when experiencing mental distress. While privacy is important at times, it's essential to seek support when struggling.

Native and Indigenous Communities[17]

Native and Indigenous communities in the U.S. are highly diverse, yet they share common cultural aspects such as a profound connection to land and nature, tightly-knit communities, strong family relationships, and traditional practices.

While these elements can contribute positively to mental health, historical oppression, and economic marginalization have created substantial barriers to accessing care for these communities. Such barriers include inadequate funding, remote locations, poverty, lack of cultural competence in healthcare providers, language gaps, and a deep-seated mistrust of the government due to its history of mistreating Indigenous communities.

The Centers for Disease Control and Prevention (CDC) has noted that Indigenous populations in America report experiencing serious psychological distress 2.5 times more frequently than the general population over a given month.[18]

---

[17] American Psychiatric Association. (2017). Mental Health Disparities: American Indians and Alaska Natives. https://www.psychiatry.org/File percent20Library/Psychiatrists/Cultural-Competency/Mental-Health-Disparities/Mental-Health-Facts-for-American-Indian-Alaska-Natives.pdf

[18] American Psychiatric Association. (2017). Mental Health Disparities: American Indians and Alaska Natives. https://www.psychiatry.org/File percent20Library/Psychiatrists/Cultural-Competency/Mental-Health-Disparities/Mental-Health-Facts-for-American-Indian-Alaska-Natives.pdf

Concepts of mental illness among Native and Indigenous communities can vary significantly. Generally, physical and emotional distress are not seen as separate entities in these cultures. While there isn't a prevailing belief in shame surrounding mental health in these communities, the entry barriers they encounter often hinder their ability to seek necessary care.

Mental Health in the Workplace and School

As we shift from discussing mental health within ethnic communities to its manifestation in various settings like schools and workplaces, it's essential to acknowledge the struggles people face due to various factors including tasks, interpersonal relationships, and expectations. These challenges can significantly hinder productivity, particularly for minorities, making it crucial to cultivate an environment conducive to open conversations, empathy, and support.

Workplace mental health care coverage has evolved significantly, transitioning from being an employment perk to a requirement, ensuring access to mental health treatment and services. With the recent pandemic serving as a catalyst, employers are increasingly prioritizing mental health, offering resources such as self-help guides, flexible work hours, shortened work weeks, and accommodations for mental health issues. They're also actively creating supportive spaces where employees can comfortably interact. Sharing personal mental health experiences, when suitable, can aid in de-stigmatizing mental health issues. It's vital to listen empathetically, offer support, and encourage professional help when necessary.

It's equally important to identify workplace elements that can negatively affect mental health, such as inadequate work-life balance, high-stress levels, and uninspiring work. Prioritizing mental health in the workplace can assist everyone in reaching their full potential and contribute to a healthier, more engaging work environment. Despite the remaining challenges, recent changes in workplace culture mark progressive steps.

Considering the significant time students spend in school, these institutions must provide comprehensive mental health services facilitating early identification, intervention, and prevention. Inadequate mental health support can result in chronic absenteeism, truancy, and disruptive behavior among students. Although many schools acknowledge the necessity of mental health resources, they often face hurdles such as insufficient funding and staffing. However, with growing recognition of mental health's importance, federal funding for these services has seen an upswing. Numerous schools have introduced DEI (Diversity, Equity, and Inclusion) and life skills programs, aiming to foster a comfortable and inclusive environment for students.

Improving mental health care in schools is a work in progress. Although it's yet to achieve its ideal state, it's undeniably improving. **As schools receive increased funding and expand services, students and faculty alike need to foster a supportive environment that acknowledges, empathizes, and effectively manages stress.**

4. Mental Health Is Non-Linear

As artist Olivia Rodrigo astutely expresses, "cause it's always one step forward and three steps back," a sentiment that can resonate strongly when contemplating mental health. There are days when you may find yourself brimming with joy and productivity, and yet, the very next day, you might feel down and prefer to do nothing more than watch Netflix in your bed. This fluctuation is entirely normal and acceptable! It might seem as if you've undone all your prior progress, but that's not the case. Remember, mental health isn't a linear process, and neither is the recovery from mental illness. Every experience, good or bad, contributes to your growth and recovery.

Case Study #1: Meredith Grey from Grey's Anatomy
Take, for instance, the character of Meredith Grey from the long-running television series Grey's Anatomy. Meredith, a surgeon, endures multiple traumatic events throughout her life - from the intense pressure exerted by her mother to hospital shootings, plane crashes, and the deaths of loved ones. Given these circumstances, it's not surprising that she experiences several episodes of poor mental health across the show's nineteen seasons (to date). She experiments with various coping strategies, ranging from avoidance of her emotions and escapism to seeking therapy.

As Meredith navigates her recovery journey, she learns to better manage her emotions. For her, channeling her grief into motivation to excel as a surgeon, mother, and friend proves most beneficial. Yet, everyone is unique, underscoring the importance of trying different strategies to navigate your mental health journey and discover what suits you best.

Take a moment to reflect on potential ways that could help you manage mental health challenges. Consider and make a note of them here. We'll delve deeper into these methods in chapter 3!

5. Severity of Emotions

According to Harvard Business Review, Americans thrive on high-intensity emotions. These emotions can be positive or negative and are felt very strongly such as anger or elation. Research shows individuals believe they need these high-intensity emotions to succeed, especially when they are in a leadership or influential role.

However, many do not realize that these high-intensity positive emotions cause the same unrest in your brain as high-intensity negative emotions. These emotions activate your body's stress response so constantly feeling them will tire your body out. Mentally, they also drain your energy. It's hard to focus when we're physiologically overstimulated since this activates the same region of our brain as a fight-or-flight response. Calming down and getting work done, however, requires you to use a different part of your brain. Therefore, in addition to the stress high-intensity emotions may bring, it also takes additional effort to regulate them.

Being pumped up or anxious are all normal feelings we experience, but if you find yourself feeling tired easily and constantly, it's probably a better idea to take a break and plan other activities throughout your day to rest your mental and physical health. This way, you can save all your energy when you need it the most!

6. Free Resources (Make Sure to Research Your Local Resources too!)

Below is a list of free resources we have complied if you would like to seek help or learn more:

- SAMHSA's National Helpline: 1-800-662-HELP (4357)
    - SAMHSA's National Helpline is a free, confidential, 24/7, 365-days-a-year treatment referral and information service (in English and Spanish) for individuals and families facing mental and/or substance use disorders.
- Crisis Text Line (text HOME to 741741)
    - Crisis Text Line is free with 24/7 support for those in crisis. Text 741741 from anywhere in the US to text a trained Crisis Counselor. Crisis Text Line trains volunteers to support people in crisis.
- National Suicide Prevention Lifeline: 988 or 1-800-273-8255
    - The National Suicide Prevention Lifeline provides free and confidential emotional support (in English and Spanish) to people in suicidal crisis or emotional distress 24 hours a day, 7 days a week across the United States. The Lifeline combines custom local care and resources with national standards and best practices.
- National Alliance on Mental Illness (NAMI)

- Today, NAMI is an alliance of more than 600 local affiliates and 49 state organizations who work in your community to raise awareness and provide support and education that was not previously available to those in need.
- Asians for Mental Health Directory
  - Asians for Mental Health was created to help Asians feel seen, heard, and empowered in their journeys toward better mental health.
- Black Mental Health Alliance (BMHA)
  - Black Mental Health Alliance hopes to develop, promote, and sponsor trusted culturally-relevant educational forums, training, and referral services that support the health and well-being of Black people and their communities.
- Latinx Therapy
  - Latinx Therapy was founded with the mission to destigmatize mental health in the Latinx community. Since then, they have expanded to become a bilingual podcast and national directory to find a Latinx Therapist (98% of our directory are Spanish speakers). Latinx Therapy strives to provide culturally grounded workshops and services to our community.
- The American Indian and Alaska Native Society of Indian Psychologists
  - The Society of Indian Psychologists' mission is to provide an organization for Native American Indigenous people to advocate for the mental well-being of Native peoples

by increasing the knowledge and awareness of issues impacting Native mental health.

7. Cheat Code Recap

1. Mental health can look different for everyone.
2. Mental health can look different for the same person on different days.
3. There is a wide range of different mental health conditions, and each condition has different sets of symptoms that can affect how we think, feel, and behave.
4. Humans experience a wide range of emotions not considered mental illness. Diagnosed mental illness is different from poor mental health.
5. Mental health looks different for different ethnic communities.
6. Good mental health is not solely the absence of mental illness; good mental health is about creating a healthy relationship with your mind, body, and emotions.
7. Mental health is not linear.

Chapter 3
Checking In With Yourself And Others

Written by: Maya Litvak, Brandon Choi, and Lilah Epstein

"I am not afraid of storms for I am learning how to sail my ship." — **Louisa May Alcott, American Novelist**

1. What Does It Mean To "Check In With Yourself and Others"?

I'm sure many of you have heard the phrases "check in on your mental health" and "ask your friends how they are feeling" but what do they mean exactly, and why are they important?

To "check in on" one's mental health simply means **to take an honest look at how a person is doing and if necessary, determine what can be done to help them improve**. This can take a wide variety of forms such as a conversation with yourself or a text message to a friend but regardless, it is a helpful first step toward being proactive in mental health.

2. How To Check In On Yourself[19, 20]

Before You Start

Checking in on your mental health may feel awkward, difficult, and daunting at first, but that's completely okay! This is a *journey* that takes some getting used to and over time, you will become much more comfortable with the whole process. One tip to keep in mind is that honesty is key! It's okay if you need some time to open up, but being as honest with yourself as possible will make this much more beneficial to you.

Starting is the hardest part, but once you sit down and check in with yourself, you'll find that the rest of it flows naturally.

Below is a list of self-reflective questions that can help spark your thought process. Including these questions in your morning or night routine is a great way to consistently check in on yourself!

---

[19]   Brantley, Ashley. "How to Check in on Your Mental Health + 7 Questions to Ask Yourself Every Day." WellTuned: Quick Tune-Ups For Your Health. Blue Cross Blue Shield of Tennessee, May 18, 2021. https://bcbstwelltuned. com/2021/05/18/how-to-check-in-on-your-mental-health-7-questions-to-ask-yourself-every-day/.

[20]   "Checking in on Your Mental Health: How Are You Doing, Really? - Choc - Children's Health Hub." CHOC: Children's Hospital of Orange County, May 17, 2021.

- How am I feeling today (mentally, emotionally, physically)?
- What's been worrying me lately?
- Am I providing my body with its basic needs?
- What am I doing to bring myself joy?
- Who do I have in my corner?

How are you currently feeling?	
Feeling great!	Keep meeting your needs and practicing self-care
Feeling good!	How can you maintain the levels you're currently at?
Feeling okay.	How can we make your day a tiny bit better?
Meh.	How can you show yourself love today? Be extra kind to yourself.
Struggling.	Practice triage. What area of your life is suffering the most right now? Focus on that one area today.
I'm empty.	Pinpoint what's draining you. Try to create a boundary and then do one thing that fills you up.

Methods

- Self-Guided Questionnaire
  - A simple list of questions can guide you along your journey of checking in on your mental health. This comprehensive method is a great starting point and can inspire other forms of self-care.
    - How am I feeling?
    - What do I need?
    - What's working?
    - What's not working?
    - What can I celebrate?
    - What can I let go of?

- Journaling
    - Journaling is a great way to reduce some of your mental burdens by transferring concerns from your mind onto paper. There are various forms of journaling such as a stream of consciousness, bullet journaling, and prompt journaling. Feel free to experiment and find what works best for you!
- Talking to a Loved One
    - Starting a conversation about how you've been doing is a great way to get support, talk about your emotions, and relieve stress. By opening up to a loved one (parent, friend, guardian, etc.), you can express yourself and strengthen your relationships at the same time.
- Meditation: Body Scan - Body Scan Practice[21]
    - Meditation is a great way to set aside time to check in with both your mind and body.
    - Body scan practices are a type of meditation that guides you through noticing different points of sensation throughout your body. You start from your head and go all the way down to your toes. This practice is particularly helpful in finding the sources of tension in your body and relieving these pressures, which in turn can allow your mind to de-stress.
    - Each meditation practice is different, and one might work better for you than another. If you're interested, try out a few different types of practices to see what works best for you!

---

[21] Bertin, Mark. "Body Scan for Kids." Mindful: Healthy Mind, Healthy Life, October 12, 2016. https://www.mindful.org/body-scan-kids/.

Case Study #1: Washington State & Mental Health Days[22]

Next, we will examine Washington State's recent law approving **mental health days**. By exploring this, we will learn what mental health days are, their importance, and how this law is changing the way we view mental health for students.

How many of you have heard of mental health days? Do your schools allow you to take mental health days?

In June 2022, Washington State passed a law that allows its students to take mental health days as excused absences.

Connection To Checking In With Yourself And Others

With this policy in place, it is now more important than ever that we know how to check in on ourselves and others' mental health. By being comfortable in doing so, we can make sure that we use mental health days effectively.

A common result of stressful school environments is **burnout: physical, emotional, or mental exhaustion that can lead to a decrease in motivation, performance, and self-opinion**. This is a concerning sign for our overall well-being. When students notice burnout setting in, taking a mental health day could be a great proactive measure to combat negative consequences!

---

[22] Azar, Kellee. "Washington Students Will Be Able to Take Mental Health Days as Excused Absences." KATU. ABC Channel 2 News, June 8, 2022. https://katu.com/news/local/washington-students-will-be-able-to-take-mental-health-days-as-excused-absences.

Case Study #2: Self-Guided Check-In Routine

Our next case study will look at the six-step **self-check-in routine** recommended by professional counselor Paula B. Martins, M.S. Ed., LPC. The routine uses various questions and practices to check in on your mental health. By discussing and participating in each of the steps, we will explore each of their benefits and how they work together to nurture our mental health.

Step 1: Breathe and Ground Yourself

The first step of this routine is to breathe and ground yourself. Take a moment, close your eyes, and take a deep breath. Inhale through your nose, feel the air expand in your stomach, and exhale through your mouth slowly. Through this practice, we aim to be present and center ourselves.

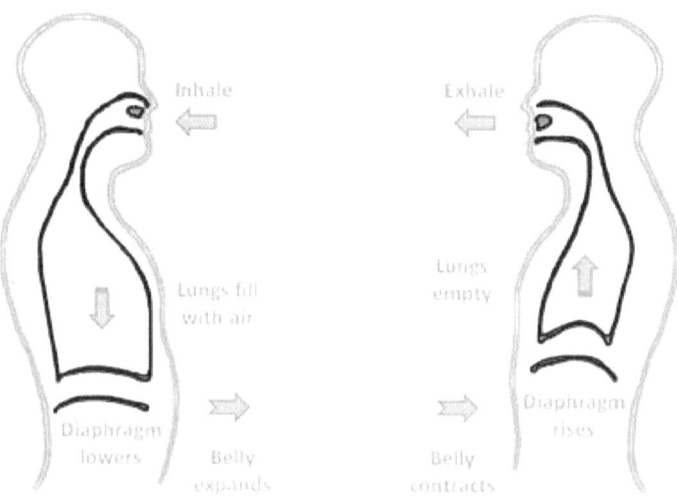

Chronic stress is a major contributor to poor mental health so we must find healthy ways to manage it. The **"relaxation response,"** studied at Harvard University in the 1970s, is a deep state of rest that can be induced through deep breathing. By beginning our routine with this step, we are restoring and refreshing our minds and body.

Step 2: How Am I Feeling?

Now that we are in a relaxed and present state, our next step is to ask ourselves: "how am I feeling?" This question turns our focus inwards and helps us reflect. This guides us to use emotional adjectives to consider our current psychological state. By doing this, we can practice analyzing our moods and expressing them in clear and concrete ways.

Useful note: when checking in on others' mental health, the question "how are you feeling" instead of "how are you doing" can help guide a more honest and helpful response. Instead of being able to brush off the question with a quick response of "I'm doing good," asking them about the emotions they are feeling can be a more beneficial conversation starter.

Step 3: Practice Gratitude

Exercising gratitude is a great way to put your day into perspective and boost your mental health. Doing this may not come easily at first, but as we practice it, it can become a powerful habit.

If there was something that reduces our stress levels, increases heart function, and boosts our emotional resilience, would you be interested? Well, practicing gratitude does all three things and more!

Research has found that by habitually noticing things we are grateful for, we can rewire our brains to have a broader perspective on life, which is more resilient to bumps in our mental health journey. This can be as simple as taking a picture of something you are grateful for, reaching out to a friend to say thank you, or even just reflecting on what you appreciate in your life. Exercises such as morning gratitude practices and 5-minute journal prompts are great places to start. Whichever method you choose to use, being consistent is key.

Step 4: What Do I Want to Accomplish Today?
When our mental health is struggling, our responsibilities and tasks may become harder to manage. Our next step asks us "what do I want to accomplish today?" By doing so, we can identify our most important goals. Completing important tasks can help us boost our mental health and achieve a sense of accomplishment daily.

For many, mental health struggles can derail responsibilities and make life seem increasingly overwhelming. By identifying tasks we want to accomplish, we can feel more organized and in control. A straightforward way we can do this is by writing to-do lists in a journal or on our phone's notes app.

Step 5: What Are My Needs Today?
Next, we identify our needs for the day.

By doing so, we use our emotional state at that moment to plan our day. This can help us treat ourselves with more patience and grace. We also become more intentional about how we choose to go about our day so we can take care of our mental health.

Many of our needs may be shared, while others may be more individualized. Here is a list of various questions that may help you identify your needs.

- How do I feel about how I'm currently taking care of myself?
- Where do I feel fulfilled (in the different categories I've picked or created such as school, work, friends, etc.)?
- Where do I feel empty or starved (in the different categories I've picked or created such as school, work, friends, etc.)?
- Where would I like to invest my time and energy (both of which are finite, i.e., precious resources)?
- What are the top three activities that bring me calmness? How can I incorporate them into my weekend, week, or month?
- What are the top three activities that bring me joy? How can I incorporate them into my weekend, week, or month?
- What activities, beliefs, and behaviors am I saying yes to that I'd like to let go?
- What activities, beliefs, and behaviors am I saying no to that I'd like to adopt?
- What boundaries do I need to set to protect my time and myself?
- At the end of each day, what do I wish I had done?

Step 6: Affirmations

Finally, we end with affirmations. Affirmations are a simple, yet powerful, method of this routine. Through affirmations, we can restore our sense of self, and remind ourselves of our competence, values, and abilities. Ultimately, affirmations are an empowering tool that enhances. Everyone likes to be affirmed in their ways, so spend some time researching your favorite affirmations and making a list for yourself!

Example Affirmations

- I am loved and worthy.
- I am open to healing.
- I am more than my circumstances.
- I am valued and helpful.
- I belong here, and I deserve to take up space.
- I strive for joy, not for perfection.
- My perspective is unique and important.
- My sensitivity is beautiful, and my feelings and emotions are valid.
- When I speak of my needs, I receive them abundantly.

3. How To Check In On Others[23]

Before You Start

Starting a conversation about mental health with others can feel a bit awkward or intimidating, and sometimes it's hard to know where to start. But before you open up a dialogue with a friend or peer, take a moment to consider the following questions:

---

[23] "Be the Friend Who Listens." Seize the Awkward. The Ad Council. Accessed June 13, 2022. https://seizetheawkward.org/.

1.   **Ask yourself:** Do I have the mental energy/capacity to help my friend? Your mental health is important too! If you're struggling, trying to help a friend might not be the best idea for either of you. And that is okay! Reach out to a trusted adult or medical professional instead.

2.   **Ask your peer:** Would you appreciate me helping you solve some problems, or would you like me to just listen and give you some company? Asking this simple question can ensure that you can help your friend in the way that they would most appreciate.

3.   **Make a note to yourself:** Remember to respect boundaries and to keep yourself open and welcoming.
     - Let your friend open up to you at their speed.
     - If they choose not to, respect their decision.
     - If they do choose to open up, respect and appreciate their bravery. The best thing you can do is be a safe and welcoming space for your friend to share.

Once you feel confident you can give another person your full support and have been assured that they would like your help, then you can begin a conversation!

Where to Start

Starting a conversation about mental health doesn't have to be complicated or daunting. It can be as simple as arranging a casual hangout with your friend. Once you're both relaxed, you can subtly steer the conversation toward their well-being by simply asking how they have been doing recently. If meeting in person isn't an option, consider reaching out via a phone call, video chat, or even a text message. It's the act of showing genuine concern and willingness to listen that truly matters.

When bringing up mental health, it is important to allow the other person to lead the conversation. By doing so, you allow your friend to decide how much they want to share, if anything at all, and avoid pressuring them to talk about something they may be uncomfortable with.

Using open-ended questions can also provide your friend with the opportunity to share their full subjective experience. It's important they understand that you want them to feel welcome to share any details, not just answering the specific questions you ask.

During the Conversation

So what should you be doing during the conversation?

Trust your instinct: when supporting a friend, consider the way you would want someone to respond if you were in their position. Your instinct might be helpful, whether it tells you to offer more advice or just simply listen.

Take the role of a listener: when a friend is in need, the desire to solve all their problems is natural. However, before coming up with pieces of advice or solutions to these issues, make sure you are truly listening to the other person. A great way to do this is to practice active listening.[24] Active listening involves listening to your friend fully engaged and without any interruptions. It can be shown through

---

[24] Mind Tools Content Team. "Active Listening Videos." MindTools. Accessed June 13, 2022. https://www.mindtools.com/aktjyjq/active-listening-video.

body language such as nodding and encouraging them to continue speaking by using phrases like "mhm" or "uh-huh." This allows the other person to complete their thoughts without any disturbances and shows you are invested in what they have to say.

Assure them of your friendship: your friend or peer might be afraid that you will view them differently after sharing certain information with you. Therefore, it is very important to assure them that you are there for them regardless of how they are doing mentally and that your relationship will not change.

Keep it casual: treat the conversation as just a talk between friends. This is not a therapy session or an interrogation, but rather a peer supporting a peer!

After the Conversation

Just because this one chat has ended, it does not mean that the conversation about mental health has to be over. Instead, continue to reach out to your friends and make sure they know they can always come to you if they're feeling down or if they ever just want to talk.

Confidentiality is a super important part of these discussions. Make sure to keep their information private and handle their trust with the utmost care. It took a lot of trust, courage, and vulnerability for them to open up, so keep that in mind and avoid gossiping or telling other people about what you heard.

These conversations can be challenging, and at times, you may feel overwhelmed by your friend's situation. It's perfectly okay to seek assistance from a trusted adult such as a parent, teacher, or counselor. Importantly, alerting someone about a friend or peer who you believe may pose a risk to themselves or others is not gossip or tattling. It's a gesture of concern and responsibility. In such instances, bringing it to the attention of a trusted adult is the correct course of action as they can ensure the individual gets the appropriate support they may need.

Not Everyone Wants To Share

Remember, not everyone is comfortable discussing their emotions. So, if a friend expresses disinterest in talking about their feelings, it's important not to take it personally. Respect their boundaries and give them the space they need. At the same time, reassure them that you're there for them if they ever decide they want to talk.

4. What Still Needs To Be Done

While strides have been made, societal stigma still surrounds mental health discussions. To normalize these conversations, continued efforts are needed. Everyone grapples with mental health in some form, and no one should feel isolated while navigating their emotional landscape.

Remember, even those who appear to have it all figured out may need a check-in from time to time. Inquiring about a friend's well-being isn't intrusive when done respectfully; it's a sign of thoughtfulness and support! In the words of Emily Coxhead, "please remember to check in on your strong friend, your busy friend, your happy friend... or your 'seems to handle everything really well' friend."

Advocating for positive change in mental health care begins with self-reflection and looking out for our friends. Let's start today!

5. Cheat Code Recap

1. To "check in on" one's mental health simply means to take an honest look at how a person is doing and if necessary, determine what can be done to help them improve.

Chapter 4
Being Compassionate Toward Yourself And Others[25] [26]

Written by: Maya Litvak, Shaan Patel, and Jumi Park

"You, yourself, as much as anybody in the entire universe, deserve your love and affection" –Buddha

---

[25]   Melwani, Shimul, Jennifer S. Mueller, and Jennifer R. Overbeck. "Looking down: The Influence of Contempt and Compassion on Emergent Leadership Categorizations." Journal of Applied Psychology 97, no. 6 (2012): 1171–85. https://doi.org/10.1037/a0030074.

[26]   Miller, Marjorie. "College Research Following Trends of Fostering Compassion for Health, Well-Being." Penn State University. Penn State News, February 8, 2016. https://www.psu.edu/news/research/story/college-research-following-trends-fostering-compassion-health-well-being/.

1. What Is Compassion?[27]

Many of us have experienced times in our lives when we've had to provide support to family, friends, or peers in a way that showcases our genuine care for them and their experiences. Similarly, there may have been challenging times when we've needed support from others. So, what do we call this?

Merriam-Webster defines compassion as "sympathetic consciousness of others' distress together with a desire to alleviate it." In simpler terms, compassion is a friendly presence during challenging times, a power that connects us despite adversity—an approach that offers support and a sense of comfort.

How individuals display and receive compassion can vary. There aren't any strict rules or methods that must be adhered to when expressing compassion, as long as it promotes a shared sense of care and understanding.

Compassion isn't limited to providing support for those around you. It also encompasses self-care: this crucial aspect of expressing compassion, called self-compassion, is about ensuring you maintain both mental and physical energy to care for yourself and others.

---

[27] Davis, Tchiki. "Self-Compassion: Definition, Examples, and Exercises." The Berkeley Well-Being Institute. Accessed June 13, 2022. https://www.berkeleywellbeing.com/self-compassion.html.

2. Being Compassionate Toward Yourself[28]

Self-Compassion

The idea of self-compassion is directly aligned with compassion in general. It involves treating yourself the way that you would treat a friend who is having a hard time. However, because we tend to be harsher on ourselves, individuals tend to find this difficult at times. The expanded definition involves three core elements[29]:

- **Self-kindness**: being kind to yourself
- **Common humility**: recognizing that everyone makes mistakes and can suffer
- **Mindfulness:** when the mind is fully attentive to what's happening, what you are doing, and the space around you

Seems simple and easy, but *why* is it so important?

As previously discussed, maintaining good mental health has numerous benefits for both the mind and body. Individuals who practice self-compassion tend to experience higher levels of happiness, life satisfaction, and motivation. Coupled with stronger relationships and physical health, these individuals also often experience less anxiety and depression. Crucially, they demonstrate the resilience necessary to navigate stressful life events.

---

[28] Mindful Staff. "How to Be More Compassionate: A Mindful Guide to Compassion." Mindful, October 4, 2021. https://www.mindful.org/how-to-be-more-compassionate-a-mindful-guide-to-compassion/#empathy.

[29] Neff, Kristin. "Definition and Three Elements of Self Compassion." Self, July 9, 2020. https://self-compassion.org/the-three-elements-of-self-compassion-2/.

In this section, we will explore methods to increase self-compassion, enhance compassion towards others, and identify when and how to seek help when a person is ready to do so. Our goal is to assist individuals in feeling more at ease with themselves and the people around them.

How To Be Self-Compassionate?[30]

We have explored the benefits of practicing self-compassion, but how does one do so? Self-compassion may appear differently for everyone; there isn't a universally applicable method. Individuals should select strategies that they find comfortable and effective. Fortunately, many of these methods are straightforward. Below are a few examples:

- Comforting the body
    - Eating something healthy or something you enjoy
    - Resting or taking a nap
    - Taking a walk or a form of physical activity that you enjoy
- Journaling
    - This can be done in many ways
        - Letter to yourself
        - Streaming your emotions (whatever is on your mind)
        - Seeing how you grow day-by-day

One important aspect of self-compassion is mindfulness. **Mindfulness**, put simply, is the basic human ability to be present, aware of where we are and what we are doing, and not overwhelmed by what is going

---

[30] "4 Ways to Boost Your Self-Compassion." Harvard Health Publishing. Harvard Medical School, February 12, 2021. https://www.health.harvard. edu/mental-health/4-ways-to-boost-your-self-compassion.

on around us. It is something we all possess and is easily accessible when we practice it.

Jon Kabat-Zinn, the creator of the research-backed program Mindfulness-Based Stress Reduction (MBSR), explains how mindfulness lights up parts of our brains that aren't normally activated when we're mindlessly running on autopilot.

There are many practices to help us be more mindful, the most popular being meditation. But other methods can help too such as mindful listening.

It can be hard to sit alone, and it can be even harder to sit alone with your thoughts, even for short periods. However, it is important to do so! Start with small increments and over time with practice, increase the length of time and become more comfortable. Try to be alone with your thoughts, have this silent conversation with yourself for five minutes a day, and then continue to do so on the following days. This routine will create more consistent results when it comes to being aware of the situation you face and the decisions you make because of it.

These are simple ways for any individual to be a little more self-compassionate- taking care of themselves in a way that makes them feel more positive as the day goes on. Doing things you enjoy and seeing how you make progress as days pass can have a positive effect on your mental health.

Using a more planned process for self-compassion works better for some individuals. Linda Graham, a resilience expert, formatted an exercise for shifting our awareness and bringing acceptance to the experience of the moment. Her technique strengthens the brain when things are tough so you can reasonably manage emotional distress. The 4-step process goes as follows:

1. Any moment you notice a surge of a difficult emotion- for instance, boredom, contempt, remorse, or shame- pause and put your hand on your heart (this activates the release of oxytocin, the hormone of safety and trust).

2. Empathize with your experience, recognize your suffering, and say to yourself, "this is upsetting," "this is hard," or any variation of these to acknowledge and show care to yourself when you experience something distressing.

3. Repeat words and phrases of validation that work for you.

4. Continue repeating these steps until you feel an internal shift: compassion, kindness, care for yourself, and becoming stronger than the original negative emotion.

3. Being Compassionate Toward Others

There are many instances where individuals may show compassion to others such as family members, friends, coworkers, or even strangers.

Revisiting the definition of compassion: a friendly presence in the face of what individuals find difficult—an approach that differs from turning away. Because these struggles are different for everyone, compassion is unique to the individual.

How to Cultivate Compassion Everyday

It is easy to find methods to show compassion to people around you daily, whether it be in the classroom, at work, or home.

In The Workplace Or School

- Take greater notice of your peers' well-being
  - It is hard to know what is going on in a person's life, especially if we don't ask.
  - If you notice someone going through a tough time, make sure to reach out. If you are not comfortable doing so, reach out to a trusted adult to do so.
- Encourage and show more positive contact
  - Use spaces for informal and planned gatherings.
  - Create more opportunities to notice when someone needs support and offer it.
- Invite more authentic and open communication
  - Keep conversations full of kindness and respect. This allows time to talk about what may need attention and an empathic connection.
- Take the perspective of the other person
  - A.k.a. cognitive empathy- simply knowing how the other person feels and what they might be thinking. This type of empathy can help in negotiating or motivating people to give their best effort.

However, compassion doesn't necessarily mean always communicating via talking or hosting gatherings to make individuals feel supported. **Even the smallest of gestures such as holding the door open for someone can demonstrate compassion towards others**.

4. Seeking Professional Help

Considering Mental Health Support

Opening up about personal struggles with mental health is difficult for many. Often, unfortunately, people face various challenges that inhibit them from starting their recovery journey. Some examples are listed below:

- People who have a hard time expressing negative feelings also have a lower motivation to seek therapy. Being vulnerable is difficult, especially when one believes it would impose a negative impression on others.
- Those who believe the misconception that mental health care is only for those undergoing severe mental disorders. This preconception can make one feel shameful, socially inadequate, and guilty for seeking help for their seemingly "normal or not bad enough symptoms[31]."

---

[31] Baptista, Makilim Nunes, and Cristian Zanon. "Why Not Seek Therapy? the Role of Stigma and Psychological Symptoms in College Students." Paidéia (Ribeirão Preto) 27, no. 67 (2017): 76–83. https://doi.org/10.1590/1982-43272767201709.

Supporting Those in Need

1. Studies[32] have shown that greater social support helps instill security which serves to encourage individuals to seek adequate psychotherapy.
2. Quality support from family and friends is a big part of mental health.
3. The physical proximity of the support group can also play a beneficial role in encouraging people to feel safer reaching out for mental health support.
4. Emphasis on the normalcy of seeking mental health professionals when you are struggling is essential to relieving any social anxiety one can have while considering psychotherapy.

Now that you have learned about some factors that prevent people from seeking help, let's look at people who advocate for mental health support!

---

[32] Baptista, Makilim Nunes, and Cristian Zanon. "Why Not Seek Therapy? the Role of Stigma and Psychological Symptoms in College Students." Paidéia (Ribeirão Preto) 27, no. 67 (2017): 76–83. https://doi.org/10.1590/1982-43272767201709.

Case Study #1: Selena Gomez's Public Support of Mental Health[33]

On May 18, 2022, Selena Gomez joined the White House to open the first-ever Youth Mental Health Forum led by the US Department of Health and Human Services and MTV Entertainment. She outspokenly discusses her support of mental health services. She promotes the Rare Impact Fund, the social effort division of her beauty brand Rare Beauty, that funds access to mental health support services for those who need it. During the forum, Selena shared that "by using my platform to share my own story and working with

---

[33] Olson, Cathy Applefeld. "Selena Gomez Joins 'White House Conversation on Youth Mental Health' Hosted by MTV." Forbes, May 19, 2022. https://www.forbes.com/sites/cathyolson/2022/05/18/selena-gomez-joins-white-house-conversation-on-youth-mental-health-hosted-by-mtv/?sh=79fcf5cb3f19.

incredible people like all of you, I can help others feel less alone and find the help they need..."

Case Study #2: Kevin Love's Mental Health Journey[34]

Competitive sports and mental health tend to not mix well. The culture around sports characterizes players as mentally and physically tough and competitive. We see players take breaks for physical injuries either minor or major, but rarely for when they suffer from mental roadblocks.

In a 2020 article for "The Players' Tribune," Kevin Love, a current player on the Cleveland Cavaliers and a 5-time All-Star and NBA champion, wrote about his mental health journey.

In 2018, when Love played for the Minnesota Timberwolves, he went back to the locker room during a game against the Atlanta Hawks. Love later shared that he left due to an anxiety attack. But this wasn't the worst he had experienced. Love described his lowest point to be during the 2012-2013 season.

Love wrote: "That's the thing that people on the outside don't fully understand. Nothing major has to happen to start a spiral. It can happen over the smallest thing in the world... And listen, I'm not trying to sell you some fairy-tale version of mental health. It took me years and years— it genuinely took 29 years for me to realize what I needed. I needed medication. I needed therapy. I still need those things now, and I probably always will."

Love acknowledged he will always live with his mental health, but after giving himself the compassion he needed, he realized it does get

---

[34] Love, Kevin. "To Anybody Going Through It." The Players' Tribune, September 17, 2020.

better and he isn't alone. From the start of his NBA career 14 years ago to now, Love has been a key figure for athletes speaking about their never-ending journey with mental health.

"I know so many people out there are suffering right now. I'm no different. I'm *still* going through it."

KEVIN LOVE

5. When Should You Seek Therapy?

Making the final decision to find a therapist can be difficult. No matter the decision you make, mental health is a personal journey. Nevertheless, it has been proven that most psychological disorders and distress can be effectively supported through psychotherapy. The following lists include who the American Psychology Association (APA) believes could benefit the most from therapy:

1. They spend some amount of time thinking about the problem every week.
2. They feel that the problem is highly embarrassing and do not want to disclose it to anyone.
3. The problem has reduced their overall happiness over the past few months.
4. Emotional difficulties have decreased the functioning of daily life, including their ability to hold a relationship and perform at their best in their job or school setting.
5. They embark on actions that are harmful to themselves or others, including overdrinking or being aggressive.

Moreover, when you notice you or a loved one feels one or more of those statements, you might also consider the next few questions.

1. Does the problem take up more than an hour of the day?
2. Have educational and professional ambitions been reduced?
3. Has the lifestyle been rearranged to cope with the problems?

If you find a "yes" to any of these questions, it suggests that psychotherapy may be helpful. Also, keep in mind that your situation may look less upsetting to yourself than to people around you.

Mental Health Is A Journey, Not An End Destination

Finding the right therapist is essential for reaping the most benefits. Remember, you may find several therapists that best fit your interests and goals. American Psychology Association (APA) outlines numerous ways to find a qualified therapist that is your best fit.

1. Ask your family and friends for any referrals. Oftentimes, this could be the fastest and easiest way to find a therapist to connect with.
2. Search your state's psychological associations. For example, if you live in Pennsylvania, refer to the Pennsylvania Psychological Association Psychologist locator website.
3. Otherwise, APA's Psychologist Locator is an effective tool to personalize your search options to various factors including location, gender, practice area, insurance, nationality, and many more.

If you find a therapist that you feel is the best fit, call and request to schedule an appointment. You could also ask any questions including their treatment plan, accepted health insurance, and their availability. Frequently, therapists offer free initial consultations to better address your concerns and to evaluate whether they can serve you.

Evaluate Your Progress Afterwards

It is *okay* to be nervous before your first therapy session! This is normal! Keep in mind that being vulnerable and forming a relationship with a therapist can be eye-opening and insightful no matter how daunting it seems.

Do not worry if you and the therapist do not connect right away. It can take a few sessions to feel comfortable or it can take a few tries before you find a therapist you like. Meanwhile, here are some questions worth asking yourself to evaluate your therapy experience.

1. Do you feel your therapy sessions consist of a dual effort from you and your therapist? If this is not the case and you

feel stuck, you should let your therapist know so they better accommodate your needs.

2. Do you feel your therapist is accepting and supportive? If your therapist appears uninterested or judgmental, you should also address this issue and potentially modify their approach or discontinue their services.

3. Are you progressing with your therapist towards the goal you hope to eventually achieve? If you feel the direction of your therapy is misguided or confusing, talk to your therapist for more clarity.

When Do I Know If I Am Done With Treatment?[35]

Unlike physical health where recovery progress is quantitatively measured, mental health recovery is not as clear. Its length varies depending on different circumstances and individuals. However, there are both quantitative and qualitative measures assessed to check your progress. The APA insists on the following factors we should be aware of:

- Both the patient and the therapist agree that the initial goal of the therapy has been accomplished.
- Research indicates that ~15-20 sessions are needed for half of the patients to recover, according to the self-reported symptom checklists.

---

[35] "How Long Will It Take for Treatment to Work?" American Psychological Association, July 2017. https://www.apa.org/ptsd-guideline/patients-and-families/length-treatment.

- ~12-16 long treatments have been scientifically shown to bring significant psychological improvements.
- Therapy sessions could extend to ~20-30 sessions (6+ months) to better ensure the installation of practices and skills learned during the treatment.
- Reminder: this all varies depending on the individual! You will work with your therapist to create a tentative plan that will best benefit you.

But remember, mental health is a journey, *not* an end destination. One might seek treatment, recover, then struggle, and seek it again. This is natural! No one can expect what life will bring us! Everyone's mental health journey is unique.

Case Study #3: BTS Speaks About Self-Acceptance And Self-Esteem[36]

On October 21, 2021, the K-pop band BTS successfully held a LOVE MYSELF campaign with UNICEF, reaching people worldwide with the message of self-care and love. As an influential group, their campaign reached 50 million engagements.

---

[36] "UNICEF and BTS Celebrate Success of 'Groundbreaking' Love Myself Campaign." UNICEF, October 5, 2021. https://www.unicef.org/eap/press-releases/unicef-and-bts-celebrate-success-groundbreaking-love-myself-campaign.
UNICEF/UN0425623/BTS and Big Hit

BTS shared: "We started LOVE MYSELF as a way to reach young people and help improve their lives and rights. During the process, we also strove to "LOVE MYSELF" ourselves, and we as a team and as individuals grew as well. We hope that many people feel how the love received from others can become the power that allows them to love themselves." The band's transparency with their personal reflections helps empower the younger generation through difficult times, especially during the COVID-19 pandemic.

Though this pandemic stagnated the whole world, its universality encouraged people to come together and face their common struggles. Unpredictable and unprecedented events happen all the time and will continue to do so. It is during those times that we should show ourselves and others compassion to feel more supported and safer within our communities.

6. Cheat Code Recap

1. Compassion is a friendly presence in the face of what's difficult, a power connecting us despite difficulties.
2. Self-compassion involves treating yourself the way that you would treat a friend who is having a hard time.
3. Showing compassion looks different for everyone and in different settings.
4. We must normalize the conversations of mental health and squash the stigma.
5. Mental health is a journey, not an end destination.

Conclusion

Written by: Maya Litvak

Thank you for reading *Inside Your Mind*. We hope you enjoyed learning about what mental health and wellness are and how they fit in and affect your and your loved ones' lives.

The concepts outlined will remain important wherever you go for the entirety of your life. We hope you have acquired the skills necessary for taking care of your mental health and can suggest them to others as well. We are optimistic that you are a part of the future positive change for the mental health field and will become advocates on behalf of yourself and others to normalize its conversations and squash the stigma! [36]

Inside Your Mind is meant to be a guide that you can return to whenever you need to revisit certain topics or need inspiration as you navigate your mental health journey. If you have any further questions, do not hesitate to reach out to a trusted adult or medical professional.

---

[36]   Cuncic, Arlin. "Why Gen Z Is More Open to Talking About Their Mental Health." Verywell Mind, March 25, 2021. https://www.verywellmind.com/why-gen-z-is-more-open-to-talking-about-their-mental-health-5104730.

The Inside Your Mind Cheat Code

Chapter 1: Mental Health & Wellness: Past, Present, & Future

1. Mental health is important for our day-to-day functioning.
2. Mental health is our emotional, psychological, and social well-being that affects how we think, feel, and act.
3. There is no single cause or simple explanation for the development of our mental health.
4. Mental health and health outcomes share a bidirectional relationship, so they affect each other proportionally.
5. Good mental health is associated with an important concept called well-being, which is the state of being comfortable, healthy, or happy.
6. The history of mental health and wellbeing has evolved over time.
7. The future of mental health is personalized care.

Chapter 2: Mental Health Has Many Shades

1. Mental health can look different for everyone.
2. Mental health can look different for the same person on different days.

3. There is a wide range of different mental health conditions, and each condition has different sets of symptoms that can affect how we think, feel, and behave.
4. Humans experience a wide range of emotions not considered mental illness. Diagnosed mental illness is different from poor mental health.
5. Mental health looks different for different ethnic communities.
6. Good mental health is not solely the absence of mental illness; good mental health is about creating a healthy relationship with your mind, body, and emotions.
7. Mental health is not linear.

Chapter 3: Checking In With Yourself And Others

1. To "check in on" one's mental health simply means to take an honest look at how a person is doing and if necessary, determine what can be done to help them improve.

Chapter 4: Being Compassionate Toward Yourself and Others

1. Compassion is a friendly presence in the face of what's difficult, a power connecting us despite difficulties.
2. Self-compassion involves treating yourself the way that you would treat a friend who is having a hard time.
3. Showing compassion looks different for everyone and in different settings.
4. Mental health is a journey, not an end destination.
5. We must normalize the conversations of mental health and squash the stigma.

Glossary

Chapter 1: Mental Health & Wellness: Past, Present, & Future

Mental Health: The overall state of our emotional, psychological, and social well-being, influencing how we think, feel, and act; a dynamic journey that evolves across our lifetime, depending on various internal and external factors

Psychological Factors: Determinants that include personality traits like optimism, extraversion, and self-esteem

Sociocultural Influences: Refers to the factors that affect social and cultural behaviors, including supportive relationships, economic status, and societal structures

Stigma: Act of viewing someone negatively due to a particular characteristic or attribute, which could range from skin color, or culture, to disability

Telemedicine: Provision of healthcare services remotely

Well-Being: A state characterized by comfort, health, and happiness

Chapter 2: Mental Health Has Many Shades

Acculturation: The extent to which an individual has assimilated to the predominant culture of their place of residence, can play a crucial role in seeking mental health care

Attention-Deficit/Hyperactivity Disorder (ADHD) Every Day Definition: Often incorrectly viewed as a "made up" disorder present only in children, assuming all individuals are either hyperactive or lazy

Attention-Deficit/Hyperactivity Disorder (ADHD) Mental Illness Diagnosis: A neurodevelopmental disorder characterized by persistent patterns of inattention, hyperactivity, and impulsivity that significantly impact daily functioning and well-being

Anxiety Every Day Definition: The often incorrectly used term to describe a state of feeling nervous or worried that something bad is going to happen

Anxiety Mental Illness Diagnosis: A mental disorder characterized by intense, excessive, and persistent worry and fear about everyday situations; often, anxiety disorders involve repeated episodes of sudden feelings of intense anxiety and fear or terror that reach a peak within minutes (panic attacks)

Bipolar Every Day Definition: The often incorrectly used term to describe a person who changes their mind or moods rapidly

Bipolar Disorder Mental Illness Diagnosis: A mental disorder that causes extreme mood swings including emotional highs and lows

Cultural Competency: The ability to understand and interact effectively with people from various cultures

Depression Every Day Definition: The often incorrectly term used to describe a feeling of hopelessness, helplessness, and sadness

Depression Mental Illness Diagnosis: A mental disorder that causes feelings of sadness and/or a loss of interest in activities you once enjoyed for at least two weeks and represent a change in your previous level of functioning; it can lead to emotional and physical problems and can decrease your ability to function

High-Intensity Emotions: The positive or negative emotions felt strongly such as anger or elation that activate your body's stress response and can drain your energy

Mental Illness: A specific condition that affects our thoughts, feelings, emotions, and our capacity to connect with others and ourselves and is diagnosed by a healthcare professional, different from poor mental health

Minority: A group that differs culturally, ethnically, or racially and does not constitute most of society

Model Minority Myth: Perception that some minority groups such as Asians are more successful than other minority students and workers, often pits minority groups against one another

Obsessive-Compulsive Disorder (OCD) Every Day Definition: The often incorrectly term used to describe an inflexible person who pursues cleanliness and routine

Obsessive-Compulsive Disorder (OCD) Mental Illness Diagnosis: A mental disorder with obsessions that are repeated, unwanted, and persistent; these thoughts or urges are often intrusive and cause distress or anxiety

Post-Traumatic Stress Disorder (PTSD) Every Day Definition: The often incorrectly term used to emphasize and/or describe an experience

Post-Traumatic Stress Disorder (PTSD) Mental Illness Diagnosis: A mental health condition triggered by witnessing or experiencing a terrifying event

Systemic Racism: Institutional racism, policies, and practices throughout a society that result in and maintain unfair advantages to some people and disadvantages to others

Victim Mentality: An unhealthy coping mechanism of a self-blame pattern that can emerge when people are dealing with past trauma or betrayal

Chapter 3: Checking In With Yourself And Others

Active Listening: The act of listening to another fully engaged and without any interruptions

Affirmations: An empowering tool that can restore our sense of self and remind ourselves of our competence, values, and abilities

Body Scan Meditation: A type of meditation that guides you through noticing different points of sensation throughout your body

Burnout: Physical, emotional, or mental exhaustion that can lead to a decrease in motivation, performance, and self-opinion, can be a concerning sign for overall well-being

Checking In: The act of taking an honest look at how a person is doing and if necessary, determine what can be done to help them improve

Chapter 4: Being Compassionate Toward Yourself And Others

Common Humility: The emotional state of being kind to yourself

Compassion (Dictionary Definition): Sympathetic consciousness of others' distress together with a desire to alleviate it

Compassion (Simpler Definition): A friendly presence during challenging times, a power that connects us despite adversity, involves common humility, mindfulness, and self-kindness

Mindfulness: Basic human ability to be present, aware of where we are and what we are doing, and not overwhelmed by what is going on around us, when the mind is fully attentive to what's happening, what you are doing, and the space around you

Self-Kindness: The emotional state of being kind to yourself

Index

1. **Mindfulness Activities:** Ackerman, Courtney E. "21 Mindfulness Exercises; Activities for Adults (+ PDF)." PositivePsychology.com, January 18, 2017. https://positivepsychology.com/mindfulness-exercises-techniques-activities/.

2. **Mental Health In Different Communities:** American Psychiatric Association. (2017). Mental Health Disparities: American Indians and Alaska Natives. https://www.psychiatry.org/File percent20Library/Psychiatrists/Cultural-Competency/Mental-Health-Disparities/Mental-Health-Facts-for-American-Indian-Alaska-Natives.pdf.

3. **Mental Health In Different Communities:** American Psychiatric Association. (2017). Mental Health Disparities: Hispanics and Latinos. https://www.psychiatry.org/File%20Library/Psychiatrists/Cultural-Competency/Mental-Health-Disparities/Mental-Health-Facts-for-Hispanic-Latino.pdf.

4. **Check In With Yourself Case Study:** Azar, Kellee. "Washington Students Will Be Able to Take Mental Health Days as Excused Absences." KATU. ABC Channel 2 News, June 8, 2022. https://katu.com/news/local/washington-students-will-be-able-to-take-mental-health-days-as-excused-absences.

5. **Stigma:** Baptista, Makilim Nunes, and Cristian Zanon. "Why Not Seek Therapy? the Role of Stigma and Psychological Symptoms in College Students." Paidéia (Ribeirão Preto) 27, no. 67 (2017): 76–83. https://doi.org/10.1590/1982-43272767201709.

6. **Methods To Check In With Yourself:** Bertin, Mark. "Body Scan for Kids." Mindful: Healthy Mind, Healthy Life, October 12, 2016. https://www.mindful.org/body-scan-kids/.

7. **History Of Mental Health:** Bertolote, Jose. "The Roots of the Concept of Mental Health." World Psychiatry 7, no. 2 (2008): 113–16. https://doi.org/10.1002/j.2051-5545.2008.tb00172.x.

8. **Check In With Others:** "Be the Friend Who Listens." Seize the Awkward. The Ad Council. Accessed June 13, 2022. https://seizetheawkward.org/.

9. **Stigma:** Bornstein, Jeffrey. "Stigma, Prejudice and Discrimination against People with Mental Illness." Stigma, Prejudice and Discrimination Against People with Mental Illness. American Psychiatry Association, August 2020. https://www.psychiatry.org/patients-families/stigma-and-discrimination#:~:text=A%202017%20study%20involving%20more,after%20one%20and%20two%20years.

10. **Check In With Yourself:** Brantley, Ashley. "How to Check in on Your Mental Health + 7 Questions to Ask Yourself Every Day." WellTuned: Quick Tune-Ups For Your Health. Blue Cross Blue Shield of Tennessee, May 18, 2021. https://bcbstwelltuned.com/2021/05/18/how-to-check-in-on-your-mental-health-7-questions-to-ask-yourself-every-day/.

11. **Check In With Yourself:** "Checking in on Your Mental Health: How Are You Doing, Really? - Choc - Children's Health Hub." CHOC: Children's Hospital of Orange County, May 17, 2021. https://health.choc.org/checking-in-on-your-mental-health-how-are-you-doing-really/.

12. **Mental Health In Different Communities:** Chou, Rosalind, and Joe R. Feagin. The Myth of the Model Minority: Asian Americans Facing Racism. 2nd ed., London, Routledge, Taylor & Francis Group, 2016.

13. **Future Of Mental Health:** Cuncic, Arlin. "Why Gen Z Is More Open to Talking About Their Mental Health." Verywell Mind, March 25, 2021. https://www.verywellmind.com/why-gen-z-is-more-open-to-talking-about-their-mental-health-5104730.

14. **Self-Compassion:** Davis, Tchiki. "Self-Compassion: Definition, Examples, and Exercises." The Berkeley Well-Being Institute. Accessed June 13, 2022. https://www.berkeleywellbeing.com/self-compassion.html.

15. **Compassion:** Former Active Minds student leader and co-creator of V-A-R®. "V-A-R: Validate, Appreciate, Refer." Active Minds. Accessed June 13, 2022. https://www.activeminds.org/about-mental-health/var/.

16. **Seeking Mental Health Support:** "How Long Will It Take for Treatment to Work?" American Psychological Association, July 2017. https://www.apa.org/ptsd-guideline/patients-and-families/length-treatment.

17. **Compassion:** "How to Check In On Your Mental Health: 5 Questions to Ask Yourself Every Day." Chester County

Hospital. Penn Medicine, May 3, 2021. https://www.chestercountyhospital.org/news/health-eliving-blog/2021/may/how-to-check-in-on-your-mental-health.

18. **Mental Health In Different Communities:** Lee, Stacey J. Unraveling the 'Model Minority' Stereotype: Listening to Asian American Youth. 2nd ed., New York City, Teachers College Press, 2009.

19. **Mental Health Support Case Study:** Love, Kevin. "To Anybody Going Through It." The Players' Tribune, September 17, 2020. https://www.theplayerstribune.com/articles/kevin-love-mental-health.

20. **Future Of Mental Health Case Study:** "Manchester Arena Bombed during Ariana Grande Concert." History.com. A&E Television Networks, May 18, 2018. https://www.history.com/this-day-in-history/manchester-arena-bombed-during-ariana-grande-concert.

21. **Future Of Mental Health:** Marcellus, Sibile. "'Stop the Shame': Talkspace, Michael Phelps, Demi Lovato Battle against Mental Illness Stigma." Yahoo! News, May 21, 2021. https://news.yahoo.com/stop-the-shame-michael-phelps-demi-lovato-and-online-therapy-platform-fight-mental-illness-stigma-124714145.html?guccounter=1&guce_referrer=aHR0cHM6Ly93d3cuZ29vZ2xlLmNvbS8&guce_referrer_sig=AQAAABbm6WZtI0sglcn0fBx02nG-eLe1zHLjoqLfQ3TMgxXhgjCqJvbi98c-x_NcPZWjxDqZWe0FAlcuDIIPJdFAOhWo2KxOEKvHHAPzXyr9H02ysgYKGq

MxpHsC8kjG2aW0BWYlz6u8D6PUEfgs4ABCHaeVmqHOa_
f5Lopl2Fb0YIoy.

22. **Compassion:** Melwani, Shimul, Jennifer S. Mueller, and Jennifer R. Overbeck. "Looking down: The Influence of Contempt and Compassion on Emergent Leadership Categorizations." Journal of Applied Psychology 97, no. 6 (2012): 1171–85. https://doi.org/10.1037/a0030074.

23. **Compassion:** Miller, Marjorie. "College Research Following Trends of Fostering Compassion for Health, Well-Being." Penn State University. Penn State News, February 8, 2016. https://www.psu.edu/news/research/story/college-research-following-trends-fostering-compassion-health-well-being/.

24. **Compassion:** Mindful Staff. "How to Be More Compassionate: A Mindful Guide to Compassion." Mindful, October 4, 2021. https://www.mindful.org/how-to-be-more-compassionate-a-mindful-guide-to-compassion/#empathy.

25. **Supporting Others:** Mind Tools Content Team. "Active Listening Videos." MindTools. Accessed June 13, 2022. https://www.mindtools.com/aktjyjq/active-listening-video.

26. **Self-Compassion:** Neff, Kristin. "Definition and Three Elements of Self Compassion." Self, July 9, 2020. https://self-compassion.org/the-three-elements-of-self-compassion-2/.

27. **Future Of Mental Health:** "New Mental Health Trends and the Future of Psychiatry." Maryville Online, 2019. https://online.maryville.edu/blog/future-psychiatry/.

28. **Mental Health In Different Communities:** Nishi, Koko. "Mental Health among Asian-Americans." American

Psychological Association, 2012. https://www.apa.org/pi/oema/resources/ethnicity-health/asian-american/article-mental-health.

29. **Mental Health Support Case Study:** Olson, Cathy Applefeld. "Selena Gomez Joins 'White House Conversation on Youth Mental Health' Hosted by MTV." Forbes, May 19, 2022. https://www.forbes.com/sites/cathyolson/2022/05/18/selena-gomez-joins-white-house-conversation-on-youth-mental-health-hosted-by-mtv/?sh=79fcf5cb3f19.

30. **Increasing Access To Mental Health Support Case Study:** Pollacco, Maya. "Ariana Grande to Give Away $2 Million Worth of Therapy." 89.7 Bay, July 6, 2021. https://bay.com.mt/ariana-grande-to-give-away-two-million-worth-of-therapy/.

31. **Stigma:** "Stigma and Discrimination." Mental Health Foundation, October 4, 2021. https://www.mentalhealth.org.uk/explore-mental-health/a-z-topics/stigma-and-discrimination.

32. **Stigma:** "Stigma, Discrimination and Mental Illness." Better Health Channel. Department of Health; Human Services, September 18, 2015. https://www.betterhealth.vic.gov.au/health/servicesandsupport/stigma-discrimination-and-mental-illness.

33. **Future Of Mental Health:** "Technology and the Future of Mental Health Treatment." National Institute of Mental Health. U.S. Department of Health and Human Services. Accessed

June 12, 2022. https://www.nimh.nih.gov/health/topics/technology-and-the-future-of-mental-health-treatment.

34. **Present Of Mental Health:** "The State of Mental Health in America." Mental Health America. Accessed June 12, 2022. https://mhanational.org/issues/state-mental-health-america.

35. **Self-Compassion Case Study:** "UNICEF and BTS Celebrate Success of 'Groundbreaking' Love Myself Campaign." UNICEF, October 5, 2021. https://www.unicef.org/eap/press-releases/unicef-and-bts-celebrate-success-groundbreaking-love-myself-campaign.

36. **Self-Compassion:** "4 Ways to Boost Your Self-Compassion." Harvard Health Publishing. Harvard Medical School, February 12, 2021. https://www.health.harvard.edu/mental-health/4-ways-to-boost-your-self-compassion.

37. **BetterHelp Case Study:** "5 Companies Offering Solutions for Employee Mental Health." RSS, April 6, 2021. https://www.artemishealth.com/blog/5-companies-offering-solutions-for-employee-mental-health.

38. **Mental Health In The Media:** "#StatusOfMind: Social Media and Young People's Mental Health and Wellbeing." Young Health Movement. RSPH | Royal Society for Public Health UK, May 2017. https://www.rsph.org.uk/static/uploaded/d125b27c-0b62-41c5-a2c0155a8887cd01.pdf.

www.ingramcontent.com/pod-product-compliance
Lightning Source LLC
Chambersburg PA
CBHW030503130626
46549CB00007B/2836